FOR THE BEST DAUGHTER IN THE WORLD

summersdale

FOR THE BEST DAUGHTER IN THE WORLD

Copyright © Summersdale Publishers Ltd, 2015

Text compiled by Elanor Clarke

Summersdale Publishers Ltd
46 West Street
Chichester
West Sussex
PO19 1RP
UK

www.summersdale.com

Printed and bound in the Czech Republic

ISBN: 978-1-84953-669-1

Substantial discounts on bulk quantities of Summersdale books are available to corporations, professional associations and other organisations. For details contact Nicky Douglas by telephone: +44 (0) 1243 756902, fax: +44 (0) 1243 786300 or email: nicky@summersdale.com.

TO..

FROM..

A DAUGHTER MAY
OUTGROW YOUR LAP,
BUT SHE WILL NEVER
OUTGROW YOUR HEART.

Anonymous

FAMILY — THAT DEAR
OCTOPUS FROM WHOSE
TENTACLES WE NEVER
QUITE ESCAPE, NOR, IN
OUR INNERMOST HEARTS,
EVER QUITE WISH TO.

Dodie Smith

A DAUGHTER IS A LITTLE
GIRL WHO GROWS UP
TO BE A FRIEND.

Anonymous

PARENTS CAN GO FROM
THE MOST WONDERFUL
PEOPLE IN THE WORLD TO
TOTALLY EMBARRASSING
IN THREE SECONDS.

Rick Riordan

YOU'LL ALWAYS BE MY BABY

CERTAIN IS IT THAT
THERE IS NO KIND OF
AFFECTION SO PURELY
ANGELIC AS OF A FATHER
TO A DAUGHTER.

Joseph Addison

CHILDREN MAKE YOUR
LIFE IMPORTANT.

Erma Bombeck

TO A FATHER GROWING
OLD NOTHING IS DEARER
THAN A DAUGHTER.

Euripides

NO MATTER HOW FAR WE COME, OUR PARENTS ARE ALWAYS IN US.

Brad Meltzer

FAME IS ROT;
DAUGHTERS ARE
THE THING.

J. M. Barrie

FAMILY LIFE IS A BIT
LIKE A RUNNY PEACH
PIE – NOT PERFECT BUT
WHO'S COMPLAINING?

Robert Brault

A MOTHER'S TREASURE IS HER DAUGHTER.

Catherine Pulsifer

I BROUGHT CHILDREN
INTO THIS DARK WORLD
BECAUSE IT NEEDED
THE LIGHT THAT ONLY
A CHILD CAN BRING.

Liz Armbruster

THE DECISION TO
HAVE A CHILD IS...
TO DECIDE FOREVER
TO HAVE YOUR HEART
GO WALKING AROUND
OUTSIDE YOUR BODY.

Elizabeth Stone

IN TIME OF TEST, FAMILY IS BEST.

Burmese proverb

HOW THE MOTHER IS
TO BE PITIED WHO HATH
HANDSOME DAUGHTERS!
LOCKS, BOLTS, BARS AND
LECTURES ON MORALITY
ARE NOTHING TO THEM:
THEY BREAK THROUGH
THEM ALL.

John Gay

CHILDREN ARE THE
LIVING MESSAGES WE
SEND TO A TIME WE
WILL NOT SEE.

Neil Postman

I WILL ALWAYS
SUPPORT YOU IN
ANYTHING YOU
WANT TO DO

CHILDREN ARE
UNPREDICTABLE. YOU
NEVER KNOW WHAT
INCONSISTENCY THEY'RE
GOING TO CATCH YOU
IN NEXT.

Franklin P. Jones

THE BEST INHERITANCE
A PARENT CAN GIVE TO
HIS CHILDREN IS A FEW
MINUTES OF THEIR
TIME EACH DAY.

Orlando A. Battista

THE INFORMALITY
OF FAMILY LIFE IS A
BLESSED CONDITION
THAT ALLOWS US TO
BECOME OUR BEST WHILE
LOOKING OUR WORST.

Marge Kennedy

MOTHERS AND
DAUGHTERS ARE CLOSEST,
WHEN DAUGHTERS
BECOME MOTHERS.

Anonymous

ALL OUR DREAMS CAN
COME TRUE, IF WE
HAVE THE COURAGE TO
PURSUE THEM.

Walt Disney

CHILDREN MAKE
YOU WANT TO START
LIFE OVER.

Muhammad Ali

WHAT THE DAUGHTER DOES, THE MOTHER DID.

Jewish proverb

IT'S ESPECIALLY
HARD TO ADMIT... YOU
MADE A MISTAKE TO
YOUR PARENTS... YOU
KNOW SO MUCH MORE
THAN THEY DO.

Sean Covey

I SEEM TO BE
HER DAUGHTER IN
INCREASINGLY
PROFOUND WAYS.

Johnnetta B. Cole on her mother

WHEN PARENTS
SAY 'BECAUSE I SAID SO,'
YOU KNOW YOU MADE A
GOOD ARGUMENT.

Anonymous

THE GREATEST PLEASURE IN LIFE IS DOING WHAT PEOPLE SAY YOU CANNOT DO.

Walter Bagehot

CLEVER FATHER,
CLEVER DAUGHTER;
CLEVER MOTHER,
CLEVER SON.

Russian proverb

THE FAMILY IS ONE OF NATURE'S MASTERPIECES.

George Santayana

AS THE LILY AMONG
THORNS, SO IS MY LOVE
AMONG THE DAUGHTERS.

Song of Solomon 2:2

YOU MAKE
ME SMILE

IF THE FAMILY WERE
A FRUIT, IT WOULD
BE AN ORANGE, A
CIRCLE OF SECTIONS,
HELD TOGETHER BUT
SEPARABLE — EACH
SEGMENT DISTINCT.

Letty Cottin Pogrebin

AND THOU SHALT IN
THY DAUGHTER SEE
THIS PICTURE, ONCE,
RESEMBLED THEE.

Ambrose Philips

YOU DON'T CHOOSE YOUR
FAMILY. THEY ARE GOD'S
GIFT TO YOU, AS YOU
ARE TO THEM.

Desmond Tutu

I ALSO BELIEVE THAT
PARENTS, IF THEY LOVE
YOU, WILL HOLD YOU UP
SAFELY, ABOVE THEIR
SWIRLING WATERS.

Mitch Albom

YOU CAN LEARN
MANY THINGS FROM
CHILDREN. HOW MUCH
PATIENCE YOU HAVE,
FOR INSTANCE.

Franklin P. Jones

AN OUNCE OF BLOOD IS
WORTH MORE THAN A
POUND OF FRIENDSHIP.

Spanish proverb

OF ALL THE HAUNTING
MOMENTS OF MOTHERHOOD,
FEW RANK WITH HEARING
YOUR OWN WORDS COME
OUT OF YOUR DAUGHTER'S
MOUTH.

Victoria Secunda

THERE IS NO CURE FOR LAZINESS BUT A LARGE FAMILY HELPS.

Herbert Prochnow

A FATHER IS ALWAYS
MAKING HIS BABY INTO A
LITTLE WOMAN... WHEN
SHE IS A WOMAN HE
TURNS HER BACK.

Enid Bagnold

YOU MAY BELIEVE IT
OR NOT, BUT IT IS TRUE,
IN THIS WORLD NO ONE
CAN TRULY GIVE YOU
MORE LOVE THAN
YOUR PARENTS.

Anonymous

CALL IT A CLAN, CALL IT
A NETWORK... CALL IT A
FAMILY. WHATEVER YOU
CALL IT... YOU NEED ONE.

Jane Howard

EVERYONE'S PARENTS
ARE EMBARRASSING.
IT GOES WITH THE
TERRITORY. THE NATURE
OF PARENTS IS TO
EMBARRASS MERELY
BY EXISTING.

Neil Gaiman

DAUGHTERS ARE
LIKE FLOWERS, THEY
FILL THE WORLD WITH
BEAUTY AND SOMETIMES
ATTRACT PESTS.

Anonymous

[WE] RAISE DAUGHTERS MORE LIKE SONS, BUT FEW HAVE THE COURAGE TO RAISE OUR SONS MORE LIKE DAUGHTERS.

Gloria Steinem

I LOVE YOU,
SO MUCH

MY GREATEST
ACCOMPLISHMENT, AND
MY GREATEST PRIDE AND
JOY ARE MY CHILDREN.
THEY TRULY ARE MY
GREATEST SUCCESS.

Catherine Pulsifer

WE'VE HAD BAD
LUCK WITH OUR KIDS —
THEY'VE ALL GROWN UP.

Christopher Morley

WHO CAN DESCRIBE THE
TRANSPORTS OF A BEAM
TRULY PARENTAL ON
BEHOLDING A DAUGHTER
SHOOT UP LIKE SOME FAIR
AND MODEST FLOWER,
AND ACQUIRE, DAY AFTER
DAY, FRESH BEAUTY AND
GROWING SWEETNESS?

George Fordyce

A CHILD CAN ASK QUESTIONS THAT A WISE MAN CANNOT ANSWER.

Anonymous

WHAT I WANTED
MOST FOR MY DAUGHTER
WAS THAT SHE BE ABLE
TO SOAR CONFIDENTLY
IN HER OWN SKY.

Helen Claes

CHILDREN NEED LOVE, ESPECIALLY WHEN THEY DO NOT DESERVE IT.

Harold S. Hulbert

THERE IS NO DOUBT
THAT IT IS AROUND THE
FAMILY... THAT ALL THE
GREATEST VIRTUES... ARE
CREATED, STRENGTHENED
AND MAINTAINED.

Winston Churchill

THE BEST PART ABOUT...
YOUR PARENTS IS THAT
NO MATTER WHAT YOU
DO, THEY HAVE TO KEEP
LOVING YOU.

Natalie Portman

HE WHO HAS DAUGHTERS IS ALWAYS A SHEPHERD.

French proverb

KIDS: THEY DANCE
BEFORE THEY LEARN
THERE IS ANYTHING
THAT ISN'T MUSIC.

William Stafford

ENJOY THE LITTLE
THINGS, FOR ONE DAY
YOU MAY LOOK BACK AND
REALISE THEY WERE
THE BIG THINGS.

Robert Brault

PUT US TOGETHER AND
WE WILL BE THE BEST
MOTHER AND DAUGHTER
WE WOULD EVER BE.

Zoraida Pesante

THE TREE IS KNOWN
BY ITS FRUIT.

Matthew 12:33

NEVER GROW A
WISHBONE, DAUGHTER,
WHERE YOUR BACKBONE
OUGHT TO BE.

Clementine Paddleford

NO MATTER HOW
OLD YOU GET,
YOU'LL STILL BE
MY CHILD

A HAPPY FAMILY IS BUT AN EARLIER HEAVEN.

George Bernard Shaw

A DAUGHTER IS A
TREASURE — AND A CAUSE
OF SLEEPLESSNESS.

Ben Sirach

FAMILY IS A UNIT
COMPOSED NOT ONLY OF
CHILDREN BUT OF MEN,
WOMEN, AN OCCASIONAL
ANIMAL AND THE
COMMON COLD.

Ogden Nash

OUR DAUGHTERS ARE
THE MOST PRECIOUS OF
OUR TREASURES, THE
DEAREST POSSESSIONS
OF OUR HOMES AND THE
OBJECTS OF OUR MOST
WATCHFUL LOVE.

Margaret E. Sangster

A LIVELY AND LASTING
SENSE OF FILIAL DUTY
IS MORE EFFECTUALLY
IMPRESSED ON THE MIND
OF A SON OR DAUGHTER BY
READING *KING LEAR*, THAN
BY ALL THE DRY VOLUMES
OF ETHICS, AND DIVINITY
THAT EVER WERE WRITTEN.

Thomas Jefferson

THE WORLD IS AS
MANY TIMES NEW AS
THERE ARE CHILDREN
IN OUR LIVES.

Robert Brault

THE FATHER OF A
DAUGHTER IS NOTHING
BUT A HIGH-CLASS
HOSTAGE.

Garrison Keillor

FAMILY IS THE MOST IMPORTANT THING IN THE WORLD.

Diana, Princess of Wales

LIKE MOTHER, LIKE DAUGHTER.

Proverb

PARENTS AREN'T
THE PEOPLE YOU COME
FROM. THEY'RE THE
PEOPLE YOU WANT TO BE,
WHEN YOU GROW UP.

Jodi Picoult

IT DOESN'T MATTER
WHERE YOU ARE COMING
FROM. ALL THAT
MATTERS IS WHERE
YOU ARE GOING.

Brian Tracy

WHAT IS A HOME
WITHOUT CHILDREN?
QUIET.

Henny Youngman

A CHILD IS A CURLY DIMPLED LUNATIC.

Ralph Waldo Emerson

HOW WONDERFUL IT
IS THAT NOBODY NEED
WAIT A SINGLE MOMENT
BEFORE STARTING TO
IMPROVE THE WORLD.

Anne Frank

YOU MAKE ME SO PROUD!

LEARN THE RULES SO YOU KNOW HOW TO BREAK THEM PROPERLY.

Dalai Lama

WATCHING YOUR
DAUGHTER BEING
COLLECTED BY HER DATE
FEELS LIKE HANDING
OVER A MILLION-DOLLAR
STRADIVARIUS TO
A GORILLA.

Jim Bishop

WE NEVER KNOW THE
LOVE OF OUR PARENTS
FOR US TILL WE HAVE
BECOME PARENTS.

Henry Ward Beecher

CHILDREN IN A FAMILY
ARE LIKE FLOWERS
IN A BOUQUET:
THERE'S ALWAYS ONE
DETERMINED TO FACE IN
AN OPPOSITE DIRECTION.

Marcelene Cox

BELOVED, YOU ARE MY
SISTER, YOU ARE MY
DAUGHTER, YOU ARE MY
FACE; YOU ARE ME.

Toni Morrison

A FAMILY IN HARMONY WILL PROSPER IN EVERYTHING.

Chinese proverb

WHATEVER THEY GROW UP
TO BE... MOST IMPORTANT
OF ALL THE THINGS WE
CAN GIVE TO THEM IS
UNCONDITIONAL LOVE.

Rosaleen Dickson

TREAT YOUR FAMILY
LIKE FRIENDS AND YOUR
FRIENDS LIKE FAMILY.

Proverb

THE TROUBLE WITH
THE FAMILY IS THAT
CHILDREN GROW OUT OF
CHILDHOOD, BUT PARENTS
NEVER GROW OUT OF
PARENTHOOD.

Evan Esar

THE HAPPIEST MOMENTS
OF MY LIFE HAVE BEEN
THE FEW WHICH I HAVE
PASSED AT HOME IN THE
BOSOM OF MY FAMILY.

Thomas Jefferson

WHILE WE TRY TO
TEACH OUR CHILDREN
ALL ABOUT LIFE, OUR
CHILDREN TEACH US
WHAT LIFE IS ALL ABOUT.

Angela Schwindt

WE ALL GROW UP WITH
THE WEIGHT OF HISTORY
ON US. OUR ANCESTORS
DWELL IN THE ATTICS
OF OUR BRAINS.

Shirley Abbott

A DAUGHTER IS ONE
OF THE MOST BEAUTIFUL
GIFTS THIS WORLD
HAS TO GIVE.

Laurel Atherton

WHEN YOU LOOK AT YOUR
LIFE, THE GREATEST
HAPPINESSES ARE
FAMILY HAPPINESSES.

Joyce Brothers

YOU CAN TALK
TO ME ABOUT
ANYTHING

AND MOTHERS ARE
THEIR DAUGHTERS'
ROLE MODEL, THEIR
BIOLOGICAL AND
EMOTIONAL ROAD MAP,
THE ARBITER OF ALL
THEIR RELATIONSHIPS.

Victoria Secunda

OUR MOST BASIC
INSTINCT IS NOT
FOR SURVIVAL BUT
FOR FAMILY.

Paul Pearsall

A DAUGHTER IS
A MIRACLE THAT
NEVER CEASES TO BE
MIRACULOUS... LOVING
AND CARING AND TRULY
AMAZING.

Deanna Beisser

HAVING A PLACE TO GO — IS A HOME. HAVING SOMEONE TO LOVE — IS A FAMILY. HAVING BOTH — IS A BLESSING.

Donna Hedges

A SON IS A SON TILL HE
TAKES HIM A WIFE, A
DAUGHTER IS A DAUGHTER
ALL OF HER LIFE.

Irish proverb

ACT AS IF WHAT YOU DO
MAKES A DIFFERENCE.
IT DOES.

William James

DAUGHTERS ARE ANGELS
SENT FROM ABOVE TO
FILL OUR HEART WITH
UNENDING LOVE.

J. Lee Thompson

WHAT GREATER THING
IS THERE FOR HUMAN
SOULS THAN TO FEEL
THAT THEY ARE JOINED
FOR LIFE — TO BE WITH
EACH OTHER IN SILENT
UNSPEAKABLE MEMORIES.

George Eliot

IF YOU CAN GIVE
YOUR SON OR DAUGHTER
ONLY ONE GIFT, LET IT
BE ENTHUSIASM.

Bruce Barton

THE HIGHEST REWARD
FOR A PERSON'S TOIL
IS NOT WHAT THEY GET
FOR IT, BUT WHAT THEY
BECOME BY IT.

John Ruskin

A DAUGHTER IS A GIFT OF LOVE.

Anonymous

WE CANNOT DESTROY
KINDRED: OUR CHAINS
STRETCH A LITTLE
SOMETIMES, BUT THEY
NEVER BREAK.

Marquise de Sévigné

OTHER THINGS
MAY CHANGE US, BUT
WE START AND END
WITH FAMILY.

Anthony Brandt

FAMILY FACES ARE
MAGIC MIRRORS.
LOOKING AT PEOPLE WHO
BELONG TO US, WE SEE
THE PAST, PRESENT
AND FUTURE.

Gail Lumet Buckley

ALWAYS KNOW,
I'M HERE FOR
YOU

IT TAKES COURAGE
TO GROW UP AND TURN
OUT TO BE WHO YOU
REALLY ARE.

E. E. Cummings

ARE WE NOT
LIKE TWO VOLUMES
OF ONE BOOK?

Marceline Desbordes-Valmore

IMPERFECTION IS
BEAUTY, MADNESS IS
GENIUS AND IT'S BETTER
TO BE ABSOLUTELY
RIDICULOUS THAN
ABSOLUTELY BORING.

Marilyn Monroe

A LITTLE GIRL
IS SUGAR AND SPICE
AND EVERYTHING NICE —
ESPECIALLY WHEN SHE'S
TAKING A NAP.

Anonymous

ALWAYS BE A FIRST-RATE
VERSION OF YOURSELF,
INSTEAD OF A SECOND-
RATE VERSION OF
SOMEBODY ELSE.

Judy Garland

I LOVE THESE LITTLE
PEOPLE; AND IT IS NOT
A SLIGHT THING WHEN
THEY, WHO ARE SO
FRESH FROM GOD,
LOVE US.

Charles Dickens on children

REMEMBER THAT
HAPPINESS IS A WAY
OF TRAVEL, NOT A
DESTINATION.

Roy M. Goodman

BE WHO YOU ARE...
SAY WHAT YOU FEEL
BECAUSE THOSE WHO
MIND DON'T MATTER
AND THOSE WHO MATTER
DON'T MIND.

Dr Seuss

IF YOU LOOK
DEEPLY INTO THE PALM
OF YOUR HAND, YOU...
SEE YOUR PARENTS AND
ALL GENERATIONS OF
YOUR ANCESTORS.

Thích Nhất Hạnh

SHE GOT HER
GOOD LOOKS FROM
HER FATHER. HE'S A
PLASTIC SURGEON.

Groucho Marx

IN EVERY CONCEIVABLE
MANNER, THE FAMILY
IS LINK TO OUR PAST,
BRIDGE TO OUR FUTURE.

Alex Haley

A FATHER IS SOMEONE
WHO CARRIES PICTURES
IN HIS WALLET WHERE
MONEY USED TO BE.

Anonymous

PARENTS CAN ONLY
GIVE GOOD ADVICE...
BUT THE FINAL
FORMING OF A PERSON'S
CHARACTER LIES IN
THEIR OWN HANDS.

Anne Frank

THE BOND THAT LINKS
YOUR TRUE FAMILY
IS NOT ONE OF BLOOD,
BUT OF... JOY IN EACH
OTHER'S LIFE.

Richard Bach

YOU CAN
DO ANYTHING
YOU SET YOUR
MIND TO!

FAMILY TRADITIONS...
HELP US DEFINE WHO
WE ARE; THEY PROVIDE
SOMETHING STEADY,
RELIABLE AND SAFE IN A
CONFUSING WORLD.

Susan Lieberman

LUCKY PARENTS WHO
HAVE FINE CHILDREN
USUALLY HAVE LUCKY
CHILDREN WHO HAVE
FINE PARENTS.

James A. Brewer

THE STRENGTH OF
A FAMILY, LIKE THE
STRENGTH OF AN ARMY,
IS IN ITS LOYALTY TO
EACH OTHER.

Mario Puzo

FAMILY IS ESSENTIAL
BECAUSE WE ALL YEARN
TO FEEL LIKE WE BELONG
TO SOMETHING GREATER
THAN OURSELVES.

Laura Ramirez

LOVE MAKES A FAMILY.

Gigi Kaeser

FAMILY IS WHAT
GROUNDS YOU.

Angelina Jolie

I HAVE THREE
DAUGHTERS AND I FIND
AS A RESULT I PLAYED
KING LEAR ALMOST
WITHOUT REHEARSAL.

Peter Ustinov

THE FAMILY IS THE COUNTRY OF THE HEART.

Giuseppe Mazzini

CHILDREN ARE LIKELY TO LIVE UP TO WHAT YOU BELIEVE OF THEM.

Lady Bird Johnson

THE BEST TIME TO PLANT A TREE WAS 20 YEARS AGO. THE SECOND BEST TIME IS NOW.

Chinese proverb

UNDER ANY SYSTEM OF
SOCIETY... THE FAMILY
HOLDS THE FUTURE
IN ITS BOSOM.

Charles Franklin Thwing

ANY ASTRONOMER CAN
PREDICT WITH ABSOLUTE
ACCURACY... WHERE
EVERY STAR [IS]. HE
CAN MAKE NO SUCH
PREDICTION ABOUT HIS
TEENAGE DAUGHTER.

James Truslow Adams

THE ONLY PEOPLE WHO
TRULY KNOW YOUR STORY
ARE THE ONES WHO
HELP YOU WRITE IT.

Anonymous

LET PARENTS BEQUEATH
TO THEIR CHILDREN NOT
RICHES, BUT THE SPIRIT
OF REVERENCE.

Plato

YOU'RE NEVER
TOO OLD FOR
A HUG

FAMILIES ARE LIKE
FUDGE — MOSTLY SWEET
WITH A FEW NUTS.

Anonymous

EACH DAY OF OUR LIVES
WE MAKE DEPOSITS IN
THE MEMORY BANKS
OF OUR CHILDREN.

Charles R. Swindoll

WE CANNOT ALWAYS
BUILD THE FUTURE FOR
OUR YOUTH, BUT WE CAN
BUILD OUR YOUTH FOR
THE FUTURE.

Franklin D. Roosevelt

CHILDREN KEEP US IN
CHECK... THEIR DREAMS
ENSURE WE NEVER LOSE
OUR DRIVE TO MAKE
OURS A BETTER WORLD.

Queen Rania of Jordan

CHILDREN ARE THE
PROOF WE'VE BEEN
HERE... THEY'RE THE
BEST THING AND THE
MOST IMPOSSIBLE THING.

Allison Pearson

THE MOTHER–DAUGHTER RELATIONSHIP IS THE MOST COMPLEX.

Wynonna Judd

DON'T LISTEN TO WHAT
THEY SAY. GO SEE.

Chinese proverb

CHILDREN BEGIN BY
LOVING THEIR PARENTS;
AS THEY GROW OLDER
THEY JUDGE THEM;
SOMETIMES THEY
FORGIVE THEM.

Oscar Wilde

HAVING A LITTLE
GIRL HAS BEEN LIKE
FOLLOWING AN OLD
TREASURE MAP WITH
THE IMPORTANT PATHS
TORN AWAY.

Heather Gudenkauf

BUILD YOUR OWN
DREAMS, OR SOMEONE
ELSE WILL HIRE YOU
TO BUILD THEIRS.

Farrah Gray

WE MUST TEACH OUR
CHILDREN TO DREAM
WITH THEIR EYES OPEN.

Harry Edwards

A DAUGHTER IS...
EVERYTHING WONDERFUL
AND PRECIOUS AND YOUR
LOVE FOR HER KNOWS
NO BOUNDS.

Barbara Cage

IT DOESN'T MATTER
WHAT STORY WE'RE
TELLING, WE'RE
TELLING THE STORY
OF FAMILY.

Erica Lorraine Scheidt

CHILDREN ARE THE
HANDS BY WHICH WE
TAKE HOLD OF HEAVEN.

Henry Ward Beecher

YOU CAN BE
ANYTHING YOU
WANT TO BE

LIKE BRANCHES OF A
TREE, OUR LIVES MAY
GROW IN DIFFERENT
DIRECTIONS, YET OUR
ROOTS REMAIN AS ONE.

Anonymous

REJOICE WITH
YOUR FAMILY IN THE
BEAUTIFUL LAND
OF LIFE!

Albert Einstein

A DAUGHTER IS THE HAPPY MEMORIES OF THE PAST... JOYFUL MOMENTS OF THE PRESENT... HOPE AND PROMISE OF THE FUTURE.

Anonymous

Meet Esme!

Our feathered friend Esme loves finding perfect
quotes for the perfect occasion, and is almost as
good at collecting them as she is at collecting twigs
for her nest. She's always full of joy and happiness,
singing her messages of goodwill in this series
of uplifting, heart-warming books.

Follow Esme on Twitter at **@EsmeTheBird**
for a daily dose of cheer!

For more information about our books,
find us on Facebook at **Summersdale Publishers**
and follow us on Twitter at **@Summersdale**.

www.summersdale.com